ALL AROUND THE WORLD
JAMAICA

by Kristine Spanier, MLIS

Ideas for Parents and Teachers

Pogo Books let children practice reading informational text while introducing them to nonfiction features such as headings, labels, sidebars, maps, and diagrams, as well as a table of contents, glossary, and index.

Carefully leveled text with a strong photo match offers early fluent readers the support they need to succeed.

Before Reading

- "Walk" through the book and point out the various nonfiction features. Ask the student what purpose each feature serves.
- Look at the glossary together. Read and discuss the words.

Read the Book

- Have the child read the book independently.
- Invite him or her to list questions that arise from reading.

After Reading

- Discuss the child's questions. Talk about how he or she might find answers to those questions.
- Prompt the child to think more. Ask: Jamaica is an island. Have you been on an island? How was it the same or different from where you live?

Pogo Books are published by Jump!
5357 Penn Avenue South
Minneapolis, MN 55419
www.jumplibrary.com

Copyright © 2022 Jump! International copyright reserved in all countries. No part of this book may be reproduced in any form without written permission from the publisher.

Library of Congress Cataloging-in-Publication Data

Names: Spanier, Kristine, author.
Title: Jamaica / by Kristine Spanier, MLIS.
Description: Minneapolis, MN: Jump!, Inc., [2022]
Series: All around the World
Includes index. | Audience: Ages 7-10
Identifiers: LCCN 2020052718 (print)
LCCN 2020052719 (ebook)
ISBN 9781636900056 (hardcover)
ISBN 9781636900063 (paperback)
ISBN 9781636900070 (ebook)
Subjects: LCSH: Jamaica—Juvenile literature.
Classification: LCC F1872.2 .S63 2022 (print)
LCC F1872.2 (ebook) | DDC 972.92—dc23
LC record available at https://lccn.loc.gov/2020052718
LC ebook record available at https://lccn.loc.gov/2020052719

Editor: Jenna Gleisner
Designer: Molly Ballanger

Photo Credits: Lucky-photographer/Shutterstock, cover; Igor_Koptilin/Shutterstock, 1; Pixfiction/Shutterstock, 3; Olga Bogatyrenko/Shutterstock, 4; CO Leong/Shutterstock, 5; Monty Rakusen/Getty, 6-7; Nuttapong/Shutterstock, 7; Photo Spirit/Shutterstock, 8-9; Rich Lindie/Shutterstock, 10-11tl; Ondrej Prosicky/Shutterstock, 10-11tr; neil bowman/iStock, 10-11bl, 10-11br; Prisma/SuperStock, 12; MyLoupe/Getty, 13; Craig F Scott/Shutterstock, 14-15; Phill Thornton Photo/Shutterstock, 16l; Fanfo/Shutterstock, 16r; Shane Luitjens/Alamy, 17; Kyodo News/Getty, 18-19; FORRAY Didier/Alamy, 20-21; Janusz Pienkowski/Shutterstock, 23.

Printed in the United States of America at Corporate Graphics in North Mankato, Minnesota.

TABLE OF CONTENTS

CHAPTER 1
Tropical Island....................................4

CHAPTER 2
Jamaica's People................................12

CHAPTER 3
Food and Fun....................................16

QUICK FACTS & TOOLS
At a Glance.......................................22
Glossary..23
Index...24
To Learn More..................................24

CHAPTER 1

TROPICAL ISLAND

Welcome to Jamaica! This is the third largest island in the Caribbean Sea. White sand beaches surround it. There are about 635 miles (1,022 kilometers) of **coastline**.

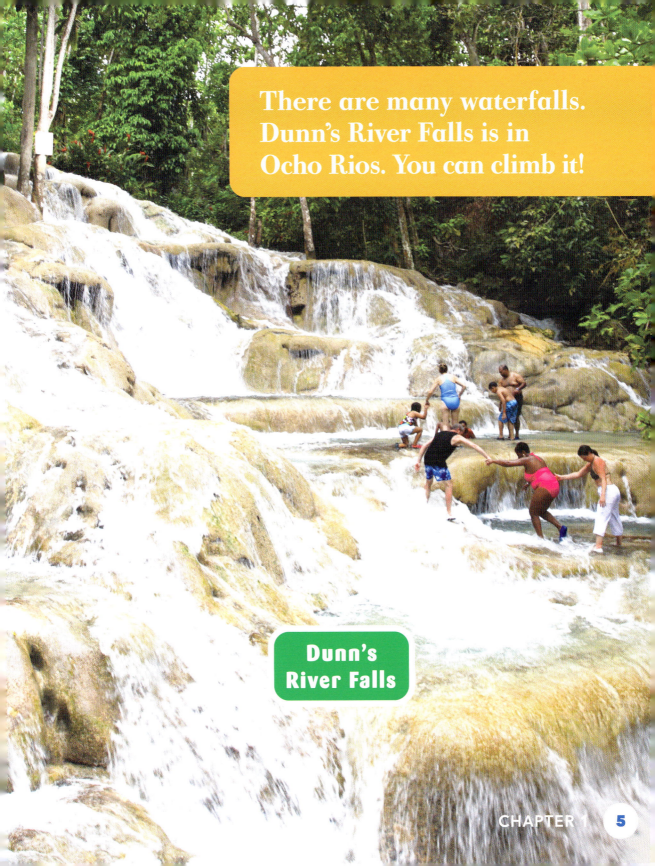

There are many waterfalls. Dunn's River Falls is in Ocho Rios. You can climb it!

Dunn's River Falls

CHAPTER 1 5

coffee beans

The **climate** here is **tropical**. Farmers grow **crops** all year. Sugarcane is one crop. Sugar is made from it. Jamaica is also known for its coffee!

DID YOU KNOW?

Bauxite is a **mineral** found on the island. It is used to make **aluminum**.

sugarcane

CHAPTER 1

The Blue Mountains rise in the east. The highest point on the island is Blue Mountain Peak. It is 7,402 feet (2,256 meters) high.

DID YOU KNOW?

Cockpit Country is a hilly region in the west. **Sinkholes** with steep sides are found here. They are called cockpits.

crested quail-dove

yellow-billed parrot

red-billed streamertail

Blue Mountain vireo

More than 25 bird **species** are found only on Jamaica. The crested quail-dove and yellow-billed parrot are two of them. The red-billed streamertail is the **national** bird. The Blue Mountain vireo makes its home in forests.

WHAT DO YOU THINK?

What birds do you see where you live? Are any of them unique to your area? Why do you think that is?

CHAPTER 1

CHAPTER 2
JAMAICA'S PEOPLE

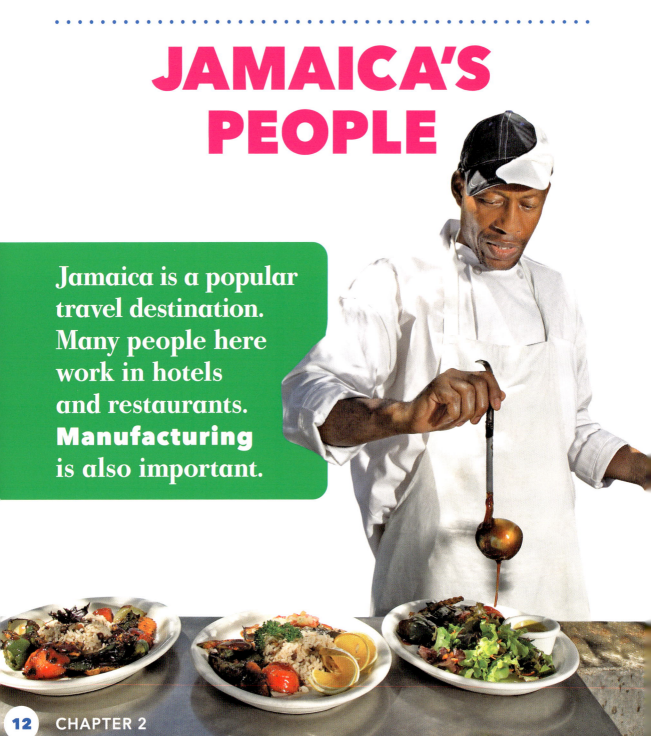

Jamaica is a popular travel destination. Many people here work in hotels and restaurants. **Manufacturing** is also important.

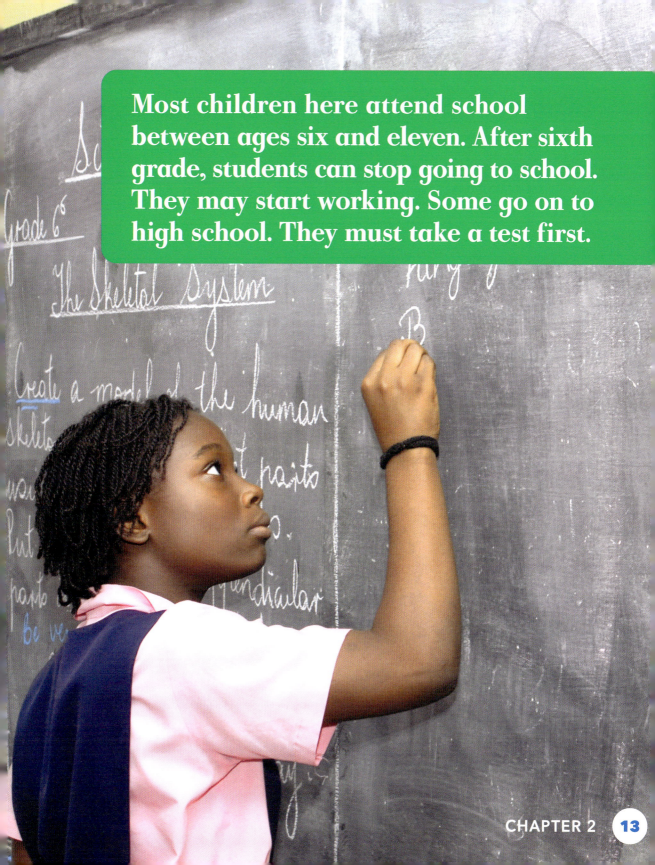

Most children here attend school between ages six and eleven. After sixth grade, students can stop going to school. They may start working. Some go on to high school. They must take a test first.

Kingston is the **capital**. People vote for members of the House of Representatives. The governor-general names members of the Senate. The **parliament** chooses the prime minister. This person leads the government.

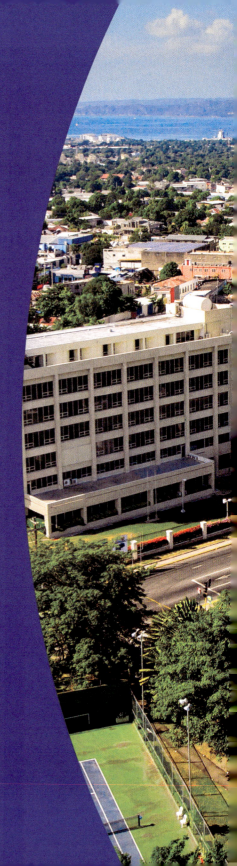

CHAPTER 3
FOOD AND FUN

Spicy food is popular here. Jerk chicken is spiced and grilled. Ackee fruit and saltfish is the national dish.

jerk chicken

ackee fruit and saltfish

Coconuts, oranges, and bananas are plentiful. Mangoes and papayas are fresh and tasty, too.

CHAPTER 3

Usain Bolt

Usain Bolt is from Jamaica. In 2016, he won his eighth Olympic gold medal. Some say he is the greatest **sprinter** of all time!

What other sports are popular here? People like to play cricket. Soccer is fun, too!

TAKE A LOOK!

The Jamaican flag is important to its people. What do the colors mean? Take a look!

- ■ = strength and creativity of the people
- ■ = sunlight and **natural resources**
- ■ = hope and **bounty** of the land

CHAPTER 3   19

Reggae music was created here in the late 1960s. These songs are about peace, love, and freedom. Steel drums add to the unique sound. Now people all around the world listen to it.

There is much to discover in Jamaica. Do you want to visit?

WHAT DO YOU THINK?

Have you heard reggae music? Did you like it? Why or why not?

QUICK FACTS & TOOLS

AT A GLANCE

JAMAICA

Location: Caribbean

Size: 4,411 square miles (11,424 square kilometers)

Population: 2,808,570 (July 2020 estimate)

Capital: Kingston

Type of Government: parliamentary democracy under a constitutional monarchy

Languages: English, Jamaican Creole

Exports: aluminum, bauxite, coffee, mineral fuels, sugar, yams

Currency: Jamaican dollar

GLOSSARY

aluminum: A light, silver-colored metal.

bounty: Something that exists in generous amounts.

capital: A city where government leaders meet.

climate: The weather typical of a certain place over a long period of time.

coastline: The place where the land and the ocean meet.

crops: Plants grown for food.

manufacturing: The industry of making something on a large scale using special equipment or machinery.

mineral: A naturally occurring substance that is gathered from the ground, usually for humans to use.

national: Of, having to do with, or shared by a whole nation.

natural resources: Materials produced by Earth that are necessary or useful to people.

parliament: A group of people elected to make laws.

sinkholes: Low areas or holes in the ground that form when soil and rocks are removed by flowing water.

species: One of the groups into which similar animals and plants are divided.

sprinter: An athlete who races short distances.

tropical: Of or having to do with the hot, rainy area of the tropics.

Jamaica's currency

INDEX

beaches 4
bird species 11
Blue Mountains 8
Bolt, Usain 18
Caribbean Sea 4
climate 7
Cockpit Country 8
coffee 7
crops 7
Dunn's River Falls 5
flag 19
food 16
governor-general 14

House of Representatives 14
Kingston 14
Ocho Rios 5
parliament 14
prime minister 14
reggae music 20
school 13
Senate 14
sinkholes 8
sports 18
sugarcane 7
waterfalls 5
work 12, 13

TO LEARN MORE

Finding more information is as easy as 1, 2, 3.

1. Go to www.factsurfer.com
2. Enter "Jamaica" into the search box.
3. Choose your book to see a list of websites.

24 QUICK FACTS & TOOLS